Trilogy Christian Publishers
A Wholly Owned Subsidiary of Trinity Broadcasting Network
2442 Michelle Drive
Tustin, CA 92780

10 9 8 7 6 5 4 3 2 1
Library of Congress Cataloging-in-Publication Data is available.
ISBN 979-8-88738-541-9
ISBN 979-8-88738-542-6 (ebook)

DEDICATION
Jesus, You are the reason that I write and sing.

To the love and joy in my life,
Ashleigh, Chloe, River, and Cowan

ACKNOWLEDGMENTS

First and foremost, Father God, Holy Spirit, Lord Jesus, You are the life in me and the breath I breathe. Without You, this book would not be.

TBN, Trilogy, Tricia Horn, Christy Phillippe, and Kaycee Thompson, thank you!

Tony, thank you.

Chloe, my songbird, for always being there for me, thank you! I love you!

Jackie Jenzano, thank you for always believing in and encouraging me!

INTRODUCTION

This is the story of how my pro-life poems came about. My family and I went to Florida on a three-day trip for Thanksgiving last year. I had previously been looking at a pro-life Facebook page and realized, first, how badly preborn babies needed a voice, and second, that there was a desperate need to combat the lies being told to women about love. Was this—society's accepted version of romantic love—one that would leave a woman alone and in a crisis? Was this the best kind of love available? Was this a cheap version of the true love women were searching and longing for? Women needed to understand there was a better way to love and be loved, and that the baby they were carrying was a person, not a choice. Jeremiah 1:5 (NLT) states "I knew you before I formed you in your mother's womb." In Psalm 37:4 (ESV), the Bible also states, "Delight yourself in the Lord and he will give you the desires of your heart."

Deciding to take God at His word, I had begun delighting myself in Him. I had been asking God to help me write songs, and specifically poems from a baby's perspective inside the womb. With Florida as our destination, after an unexpected eight-hour delay, we boarded the plane. Sitting in the window seat with my pink marker and new notebook in hand, I was expecting to write. In Numbers 23:19a, the Bible states that God is not a man that he should lie. If He said it, He will do it. Usually on our summer vacation flights, I'm all about the snacks. When the stewardess is handing out refreshments, I will ask for the works: the cookies, the pretzels, and a whole can of my favorite, ginger ale. This flight was different. I had not one bite of anything, nor did I enjoy my usual can of soda. So, praying quietly in my window seat, I read a couple of scriptures, and ideas started surfacing. After writing each poem, I would hand the notebook to my daughter for her opinion. After receiving positive feedback from her, I would rewrite each poem from the rough draft. After I had written seven poems, the pilot announced we were preparing for landing. I jokingly said, "Can't we circle another hour, so I can keep writing?!" Looking back now, I think God had us take that trip to get me to sit still long enough to hand the poems to me.

"I knew you before I formed you in your mother's womb."
Jeremiah 1:5 (NLT)

3

Table of Contents

Mommy and Me

The love between my mommy and me
Could only come from God, you see
It's innocent, it's pure, it's cuddly, secure
Only Mommy's not sure there's room 'nuff for me
God's plan for Mommy included love I could bring
Would make her laugh, cry, and sing
The love between Mommy and me

Gone Too Soon

Gone to heaven
Oh, too soon
Deadly choices
Made in ruin
A bundle of laughter
Giggles and love
Now held in the arms
Of heaven above

Maybe Someday

In the arms of Jesus
Content will I be
Until the day
I get to meet
Maybe my daddy
Maybe my mom
Maybe a family we'll be
Until then I dream of someday

Deciding to Let Me Be Me

If I were deciding to let me be me
I would think of all the possibilities
If allowed to be born
Would I be shy or toot my own horn
Would I be little
Would I be big
On my big arrival day
Would I be quiet or dance a jig?
Oh, the possibilities
If I could
Just
Be
Born

Baby Inside

Oh, baby inside
Soon will not be able to hide
What will I choose
If baby lives, will I lose
God, help
Can't decide
My deciding to engage in the physical welcomed baby within
Oh, to go back to decide again
Now will I choose to take away life
Or will the life I save be baby's and mine

Lost and Searching

Drinking and driving
Lost and searching
Empty, thirsty souls
From guy to guy
Hoping somebody shows
To you the love you're desperate for
Only to find your heart dropped to the floor
By empty promises of this, that, and the other
When seeking love turned you into a mother

I knew you before I formed you in your mother's womb.

Jeremiah 1:5 (NLT)

God Knew Me

God knew me before formed in
My mother's womb
Once a place of safety
Some have now made a tomb
There's a sparkle in my eye
I wish you could see
Will you choose life
Or is this it for me
Choose life Mom
Choose life Dad
Give me the chance you've had
Letting me live will have
Its challenges and trials
If even you knew me
For just a little while
You would see
I have Dad's eyes
I have Mom's nose
I pray I'll not yet
To heaven go
Once in your arms I'll know
Life is what you chose

Little Hands

Little hands and little feet
Somersaults and hiccups
Hiccups and somersaults
And sucking on his thumb
What will you look like
When you are one
If allowed to be born
Who will you become
How blessed are the
One-day-olds
Allowed to have been born
Allowed to have been born

Lost Get Found

Little baby, little baby
From where did you come
From heaven above
The true source of love
Little mother, little mother
Are you lost or are you found
Come to Jesus
All who are burdened and bound
It's how the lost get found

Little Star

Little star shining bright
Won't be coming out tonight
Too much fear
Too much fright
Shushed a light out
Out of sight
Off to heaven here we go
In the arms of heaven to hold

Imperfectly Mine

Perfect little hands
Perfect little feet
Who will you be when we meet
What if what I see isn't perfect at all
What if my baby has flaws
God, I trust you with all of my heart
I know You have been with me
All the way from the start
Your life You have given
So that we're cleansed, healed, forgiven
This baby now you have gifted to us
Grant us mercy and grace
To live up to your trust
To nurture and raise
In love and admonition of You, Lord
As we give this child back to you
May we train him up in the way he should go
When he is older
I pray that he knows
He was bought with a price
A life's sacrifice
I pray he lives a life
Pleasing in Your sight

Heaven Help

Heaven help us
Heaven hear
Look upon us
Please stay near
We have started something
Not sure why
Which has made
This land cry
Crying from bloodshed
Crying from fear
Decisions made for convenience's sake
Affecting us for years
Temporary situations
Ending in permanent decisions
Heaven help us
Heaven hear
Look upon us
Please stay near

Truth Uncovered

Why would they lie
Why would they deceive
Why lead one astray
When one had conceived

The evil one is roaming
Seeking whom he may destroy
Don't be caught unaware
That too would be his ploy

To convince the world
He doesn't exist
Praying he'd be stopped
Though he longs to persist

He can't get to God
So he tries to kill man's seed
Believing his lies
Only helps him succeed (temporarily)

A battle is on
A battle rages
To keep addictions going
Minds locked in cages

He tries to convince
That sin is okay
What you must realize
Is there's a better way

A mighty warrior
The Prince of Peace

Laid down His life
For you and for me

Offering peace, hope, and love
Joy overflowing
If only you knew
You would certainly get going
Run, run, running
To the One who saves
Heals and delivers
From all of the rage

Run to the cross
Drop to your knees
Kneel before a King
Who has everything

All you could want
All that you need
Peace, hope, and joy
In a world full of greed

Come to the water
Taste just how sweet
My Jesus is truth
In a world of deceit

Time to shed the old
Time to put on the new
Let go of the past
And let Him renew

He offers a refreshing
Down deep in your soul
Don't let this moment pass
Before giving Him your all

There will be an exchange
Truth for lies
Joy for pain
Peace for despair

A cleansing away of shame
It's time
Today is the day of salvation

Hats

Hats, hats
Who wears hats
We all wear hats
It's where it's at
Which hat do you wear
Are you a mother, a daughter, a friend
Are you a lover
A husband, a wife
God's Word states that we are to
Do all things decently and in order
If I am to put on and wear the hat of someone I'm not
Taking hold of something or someone before it's time
What if I didn't want to wait
What if I had the chance to explore
Knowing what God says about it
But my choosing to ignore
What if I chose to touch someone who is not mine
Would it really be that bad
Would it really be so wrong
Everyone's doing it
Joining in on the fun
What we must realize
If we really understood
We would run, run, run
Away from the shadows dancing underneath the door
Looks like a party
Looks like a blast
It's called seduction
If you could see it for what it is
You would run really fast
Away from the steal, kill, destroy plan
Of one who's called Satan

The enemy of our soul
Who longs to take from you
Your breath
Your joy
Your life

Your all

Look to the one
Who gave His all
So that you could have
Peace
Joy
Forgiveness
A fresh start
A clean heart
Hats
Take off the hat of
Everyone else is okay with it
Put on the hat of newness of life
And when the time is here for you to wear the hat you are longing to wear
You will do so with
Zero guilt
Zero regret
Zero emotional pain
With God, there are no losses
Just everything good to gain

New Life

As I walk through this life
Sometimes in joy
Sometimes in strife
I know God is there
To grant me new life

It's there for the asking
A gift that is free
He sacrificed His son
Did it all for you and me

In times of loneliness
In times of despair
These are the times
He is most near

Holding me as I call out
Crying in pain
This broken world's seduction
Can bring such shame

I cry to my Father
Falling onto my knees
He lifts my chin
To say I am here
Lifting from your shoulders
Your burdens and pleas

I love you, Lord
With all of my heart
Knowing You have been with me
All the way from the start

You knew me before
Formed in my mother's womb
Plans You have for me, Your child

I pray they resume

Consume me, Lord
Burn away what's not of You
I'm done with the old
Ready for the new

My heart is yours
It's yours to keep
I lay it all down
Lay it down at Your feet

Use me, Lord, for your purpose and plan
I am Yours right here
Right here where I stand
I am fully convinced
You are
The Great I Am

A Song My Oxygen

When all I want to do is run
Away from troubles of life
Running to this or to that
Trying to forget the strife
Would do better to remember

Jesus, You're my oxygen
Lifting my voice to sing
Giving hope and life breathing

Lord, you are the love
The oxygen I breathe
No need to run
No need to hide
All I hunger for and need

I sing and worship, melt in your embrace
In this hard life
You, Jesus, are my oxygen
You, Lord, my sweet escape

Longing for the day
When I see Jesus face-to-face
Longing for His all-encompassing embrace
Never letting me go
He's all I want to know

Lord, show me all I should be
Show me the You inside of me
Until all I am
All I have
To give

To them
Is You

To this lying
To this dying
Lost
Broken
Empty
World

Hold my hand
As I hold theirs
Let me be the love they need
As I lead them to
The Way
The Truth
The Life that You are

1

The Wrong Kind of Love

If a girl ends up pregnant by a guy she is not married to, is that part of the love one receives in our modern day boyfriend/girlfriend relationship? Is this really the love she was wanting or needing? Of course not, but pregnancy is a direct possible outcome of the physical act of sex—an act that some have wrongly labeled love. It has been said that sometimes women will give sex to get love, and sometimes men will give love to get sex. If that is true, let's break down what is being exchanged to better understand what is happening.

Let's start here. If a guy will give love to get sex, what is he doing that is being identified as love? Sometimes, a guy will say all the right things he thinks a girl wants or needs to hear. He may tell her she is pretty or beautiful or that she is everything he has ever wanted. Now, compliments are great, but not if they are part of a manipulative plan. If a guy is giving to get something, then maybe the thing he is giving isn't genuine, nor is it really what a girl wants or needs.

What about the physical side of things? How would a guy show love to a girl physically? He might touch her hair, hold her hand, hug and kiss her. Or at least try, right? Again, if someone is giving to get something, then should we really trust what's being given? It has been said that love gives, but lust takes. Another way to say it would be that love always does what is best for another.

Conversely, lust is selfish, caring for its own needs and satisfaction. Regarding the physicality of boyfriend/girlfriend relationships, the "letting a guy touch you" aspect of what society deems normal should really be off-limits anyway, whether his intentions are pure or not. Sex in all its glory has to do with more than the physical act. There is something called foreplay, which is—if I can put it this way—"playing before" to set the mood or to prepare one for the act of sex. All parts of sex, before, during, or after, are meant for marriage, period. Why such an adamant point of view?

Have you seen the live action Disney movie Cinderella? There's a part in the movie, at the castle, when the prince touches Cinderella. Now, I know this is only a movie, but don't they say art imitates life? His touch affects her breathing! She quivers at his touch! Physical contact is powerful! This physical interaction is created by God to bond a couple together in marriage.

Have you ever wondered why people who have been cheated on, or even abused, choose to stay in the relationship? They most likely had taken part in emotional or physical bonding, or both, causing soul ties to form. Sex doesn't just affect the body. It involves the mind, the will, and the emotional part of a person. Even after simply spending hours together talking on the phone, some couples find they feel a strong connection or bond.

Others have wanted to protect themselves from close attachments to someone of the opposite sex until they are seriously considering a future with that person. This is where courtship can be helpful. Courtship protects one from emotional attachments with someone they may not have a future with. Courting would not be spending long hours one-on-one with someone, again, until they are seriously considering them to be a potential life partner and spouse. Courting provides protection against one-on-one dating, where the temptation for physical closeness can become too real. It protects against premarital sex.

If someone's intentions are not completely pure, and they are trying to engage in a behavior or act that is not theirs to engage in at this stage of "the game" (being unmarried), sex isn't something that one should be involved in. Before marriage, a person needs to see clearly and not have their mind clouded by emotional ties that being involved in sex can bring. Sex is a gift given by God, our Creator, to be enjoyed in marriage.

In the Bible, when it mentions that a couple had been involved in sexual relations, it states of the man that he knew her. There is an element of mystery between a couple before they engage in sex. There have been stories told about one-night stands. It has been said that once some guys "get" a girl, or experience a girl sexually, that they are on to the next. Could it be that an element of mystery was given away to someone that should not have been? This sharing of one's self, the good, the bad, a person's all—why would one want to give such a personal and intimate part of themselves to someone who may only be in it for the kicks or for the sake of the conquest? The showing and giving of one's all to someone in sex is meant for the couple who have joined each other's lives at the altar, who have fully committed themselves to each other before God and man in holy matrimony.

Sex is meant to be enjoyed and explored by a married couple. Sex is for procreation as well as physical and emotional enjoyment. If we are to be completely honest with ourselves, the premarital touching is where the "waters of understanding" tend to be more than a little mucky. There are lots of opinions out there. Some are of the mindset that it's okay to side hug, or it's okay to kiss, if the "boundaries" are respected or aren't crossed. Taking physical and emotional passion to the edge is like driving a race car and testing just how close one can get to the edge of the cliff without going over. Passion is powerful and shouldn't be tested. Sex before marriage is like opening Christmas presents (shhh.... secretly) before it's time, only to find that the secret holders who had opened the gift earlier than the designated time had only cheated themselves.

Have you ever planned a vacation and found that the countdown and anticipation can be almost as exciting as actually being on vacation? This is another reason to wait for sex. In Psalm 84:11b (ESV), God's word states: "No good thing will he withhold from them who walk uprightly." We either take God at His Word, or we don't. God's Word also states in Matthew 6:33, "But seek ye first the kingdom of God and his righteousness; and all these things shall be added unto you."

There are consequences to going against God's good plan for us. When a couple breaks up after having been sexually active, there is a real emotional pain that is to be dealt with after having bonded and then separating. Pain can sometimes be a good teacher, even though this kind of breakup can carry with it a hit to one's self-esteem and self-worth.

Even still, the painful experience is a clear indication that something is not working. The part that is not working is part of Satan's steal, kill, and destroy plan. First Peter 5:8 states, "Be sober, be vigilant; because your adversary the devil, as a roaring lion, walketh about, seeking whom he may devour;" What better way to render someone ineffective in one's life than to hit them right in the center of their self-worth?!

I have heard there's a new way of breaking up now. It's called ghosting, where one isn't even given the dignity of being told that the person doesn't desire to be in relationship with them any longer. Ouch! There is a better way! It's the only way to peace, hope, and love—true love, pure in mind and body. The only way to have a pure heart and mind resulting in a pure life is to follow God's instructions and to conform ourselves not to this world, but to cleanse our minds by washing and keeping it clean with the Word of God.

The Bible clearly states in Proverbs 4:23 (NLT) that we are to "guard our heart above all else, for it determines the course of our life." Essentially, we are what we take in. I once watched a movie back in the day, before trying to live a life of integrity, that had an alarming amount of swearing in it. Well, you may have guessed, I came out of that movie with a vocabulary I was not proud of. Talk about "garbage in, garbage out!" The Bible states in Galatians 6:7, "Be not deceived; God is not mocked: for whatsoever a man soweth, that shall he also reap." Psalms 101:3 (KJB) states, "I will set no wicked thing before mine eyes." Psalm 119:9 (NIV) states: "How can a young man stay on the path of purity? By living according to your word."

Success in this area will only happen when we feed our spirit man the Word of God. The Bible states in John 6:63 (NASB) that "it is spirit who gives life; the flesh provides no benefit; the words that I have spoken to you are spirit and are life. Galatians 5:17 (CSB) states, "For the flesh desires what is against the spirit, and the spirit desires what is against the flesh; these are opposed to each other, so that you don't do what you want." So, does this mean we fight a losing battle? It means we are in a battle. One's thoughts determine one's actions. So our thoughts need to be clean. When we read the Bible, the Word of God, it cleans the mind. When we feed our spirit man the fuel of God's Word, it sets the mind right.

What if God allows success in this life, only if we live a life pursuant and in obedience to Him? Sure, we see people every day, like celebrities for instance, that do not live according to God's Word, yet they have what this world calls success because they have financial riches. Many wealthy professional athletes' and celebrities' lives have been cut short due to overdosing on drugs. Money, in all its glory, does not bring fulfillment in this life. Each one of us were created with a God-shaped void that only He can fill. In this life, one can only find satisfaction and true contentment in Him.

2

The Choice of Life or Death

Deuteronomy 30:15-16 (BSB) states, "See, I set before you today life and goodness, as well as death and disaster. For I am commanding you today to love the Lord your God, to walk in his ways, and to keep his commandments, statutes, and ordinances, so that you may live and increase, and the Lord your God may bless you in the land that you are entering to possess." Think about it and ask the question, "Why am I here?" Ephesians 2:10 (NIV) states, "For we are God's handiwork created in Christ Jesus to do good works, which God prepared in advance for us to do."

Have you ever behaved in a way that was embarrassing or against everything you believe in? It didn't feel too good, did it? Living right doesn't just have its rewards. It feels good within one's spirit to do so. Have you ever noticed when someone is guilty of doing something wrong, whether it is a lie or they had stolen something, their entire demeanor changes. Their eyes start to shift from side to side. They may even act a little antsy or uncomfortable.

We were made for a purpose. Going against that purpose and living in a way that goes against God's way of living causes emotional and physical distress to ourselves. God offers more than rules and regulations. He has guardrails to keep us safe in this life. His way of living will keep us blessed, happy, content, and satisfied. Psalm 1:1-3 (NLT) states, "Oh the joys of those who do not follow the advice of the wicked, or stand around sinners, or join in with mockers. But they delight in the law of the Lord, meditating on it day and night. They are like trees planted along the riverbank, bearing fruit each season. Their leaves never wither, and they prosper in all they do."

What will you choose? I pray you choose life and His way of living, so that you can truly be happy, content, and satisfied.

3

Living with Integrity

Psalm 84:11b states, "No good thing will he withhold from them that walk uprightly." It can be quite challenging sometimes to keep our word, to let our words and actions match. Nothing that is worth having ever comes easily. Being a person of integrity can especially be difficult when we constantly see others not displaying it in their lives. For instance, imagine you're in a quiet movie theater, and you hear the echo of a pop can opening, and you know full well they do not sell that item at the concession stand. Or maybe you are driving on the expressway, and cars are passing you as if you're not even moving. The way that I like to think of it is that those who are speeding or sneaking in concessions may or may not already be established in their career, they may or may not already have that record deal, or they may or may not have signed the papers purchasing their new home. If I want to have favor in my life, then I will need to live in a way that is honoring God. Each upright decision, and move on my part, means that I am one step closer to having my plans brought to fruition. Every time I decide to do what's right, I am one step closer to my plans being established. Every time I drive the speed limit, as I am waving to and well-wishing those speeding by, I am that much closer to my accomplishments.

By the way, it feels a lot better doing what is right. That in and of itself is a reward. And when you're driving the speed limit, you won't have to wonder if the police are around to catch you speeding on their radar gun. You can just relax and know that blessings are on the way to you because Psalm 84:11b states, "No good thing will he withhold from them that walk uprightly," and Numbers 23:19 states, "God is not a man that he should lie." Trust in that.

4

Getting Healthy and Emotional Hunger

Be honest with yourself and identify what may be missing. Reaching for the wrong things in this life to satisfy one's hunger can often lead to trouble physically, spiritually, or emotionally. If we had been driving for long hours on a road trip and had happened to see a restaurant, realizing our stomachs were empty, we would probably stop to eat, especially if we had missed a meal. Many people today are dealing with a craving in their souls, and as a result, they're reaching for things to fill the emptiness. It's almost like people are living their lives as if they've "missed a meal." Different things can cause a void. Many have found themselves experiencing a sense of loss for one reason or another.

One thing that may cause this sense of loss or void is a father that has been missing either from separation, divorce, or from the death of a loved one. Only God can replace the love of a father. Psalm 68:5 states that God is a Father to the fatherless. The thing is, some try to fill the emptiness with things that simply cannot fill those areas or needs. If you have lost a father or he has been missing in your life, a healing needs to take place, so that there is not a continual search, attempting to fill that place of loneliness. God can fill this need. Again, He is a father to the fatherless, a friend who sticks closer than a brother. The Holy Spirit is a gentleman, though, and will not force Himself on anyone. He just needs an invitation. God is willing to fill the empty space inside that only He can fill. He gave His all, proving His undying love, when He sacrificed His one and only Son for you and for me. Just receive Him by asking Him to come into your heart. When you do, you will never be the same.

5

Physical Hunger

For those who have struggled with weight, reaching into one's bag and conveniently finding a bag of chips or a candy bar is only going to cause the battle of the bulge to continue.

Have you ever heard the phrase, "Resist the devil, and he will flee?" A good strategy can be to "identify" the enemy. Am I saying a bag of potato chips is from the enemy? Maybe. Okay, maybe not. But let's not be our own worst enemy!

What if we were to act on behalf of a "trainer" for ourselves? You've probably seen TV shows where celebrities have hired a nutritionist or personal trainer, only to have them throw all of their favorite junk food right into the trash. That might not be that bad of an idea. Exercise (approved by a physician, of course), carrying healthy snacks, and being honest with ourselves is truly the only way to get real results.

6

Looking for Love in All the Wrong Places

From the outside looking in, a boyfriend/girlfriend relationship might seem to be something special. Just like looking at a closed door and only being able to see casted shadows dancing from underneath that door. It looks like a party! It looks like fun! It looks like something I'd like to be doing!

The thing is that many times what we think we see isn't what is going on. For instance, we may see a girl holding her boyfriend's hand. She may be laughing, smiling, and seemingly happy, and I'm sure some are.

There are also those who may very well be experiencing pressure to fulfill her boyfriend's physical needs. Laughing and smiling her way through might be the way she keeps from revealing what's really going on. Pressure to be sexually active is real. In a world of "I want it, and I want it now," and in a society that isn't embarrassed by its violent video games and overtly sexual music videos, things have gone off the rails, but few are speaking about it. Isn't it time the truth be told? Isn't it time we moved the curtain to reveal what the deceiver is trying to do?

34

7

Mistakes and Wrong Moves

Have you ever made mistakes? Of course, we all have. Some mistakes or decisions have greater, more serious consequences than others. Most would admit to having a lapse in judgment at one time or another. Then there are other mistakes or wrong moves that some tend to struggle with, where that certain thing is done over and over, almost like it's against their will. Hebrews 12:1b (NIV) states, "Let us throw off everything that hinders and the sin that so easily entangles. And let us run with perseverance the race marked for us." There are things called strongholds, or generational curses, that need to be torn down in Jesus's name and surrendered to God.

8

Things to Surrender and Doors to Close

If I have a history of dealing with fear, then horror movies may not be something I want to fill up on. In fact, I may want to completely close the door on that. If I've been struggling with lust, I may want to choose entertainment (movies, music, etc.) with protecting myself in mind. I once had a friend back in the day that declared he was no longer going to see movies rated PG-13 (or worse) after having seen a PG-13 movie that ended up being perverted. He later went on to be a youth pastor before eventually becoming a senior pastor.

When all is said and done, we all want to love and be loved. Our Creator and God loves us. Psalm 139:17-18 (NLV) states, "How precious are your thoughts about me, O God. They cannot be numbered! I can't even count them; they outnumber the grains of sand!" Luke 12:7 (NLV) states, "And the very hairs we have on our head are all numbered." The One who paints the sunrise, the One who paints the sunset differently each day, is the same ultimate artisan who made you and me with our own unique laugh, smile, and personality.

Sometimes hearts break, and tears fall in this fallen, broken world that we live in. Psalm 56:8 (AMP) states, "You have taken account of my wanderings; Put my tears in your bottle. Are they not recorded in your book." Have you ever known anyone who loves the way that God loves? Know this: you are truly loved.

9

The After-Party Hangover-Preventing Supplement

Once, in line at the register of a grocery store, there were two college-age girls in front of me. I had noticed one of the few items they were purchasing was an over-the-counter hangover-prevention supplement. They had been carrying on a friendly conversation with the cashier, so I felt comfortable enough to speak to them. I asked one of the girls, respectfully, if she could check the label on the side of the package for me. As I was speaking, she picked up the item. I continued to ask if the label on the box stated that that product prevented a broken heart. With a slightly confused look on her face, she looked at me, then she looked at the label on the box. Of course, I knew that wouldn't be listed on the label. I just wanted to make the point to this young lady, that after an evening of drinking and partying, a hangover is sometimes the least of one's concern.

37

10

A Right to Choose

I have the right to choose to engage in sex without having all my ducks in a row—no house of my own, no finances, no supportive spouse to help care for and provide for a baby should I get pregnant. It takes two to make a baby. It takes two to care for and raise one. Question: Why would I put myself at a disadvantage by giving my all to a guy if he hasn't given his all to me? Why would I put myself at risk for pregnancy? If I get pregnant, my belly grows. His doesn't. If he is not committed to me in the eyes of the law and before God, He can walk away while I must deal with the consequences of my actions. Is sex really that important to risk STDs or an unplanned, unprepared for pregnancy? No, not this way.

Sex is a gift given by our Creator to be opened at its proper time within the protected covenant of marriage. If one places fire outside a fireplace or fire pit, one will get the same result that sex outside of marriage brings. If you are willing to take that chance, with the mindset of 'It's okay if I get pregnant. I'll just end his or her life. I'll just terminate the life growing inside,' then be willing to live with the consequences of those actions. There is damage to be dealt with. It's Satan's steal, kill, and destroy plan. Every choice made that is contrary to God's way is essentially cooperating with the steal, kill, and destroy plan of the enemy. Yes, he's real. It's all in the book of truth, the Bible. Killing destroys a life. It takes away peace and emotional stability. It's breaking God's thou-shalt-not-kill law (Exodus 20:13). Sex outside of marriage is just dumb! It puts a girl at a disadvantage with a guy. If a guy loves a challenge, keep him challenged until marriage! Stop cheating him of the thrill of the chase! Stop cheating yourself out of a healthy life and future. Wait! You are worth it! I know we sometimes make mistakes, but there is forgiveness, a second chance, and a starting over.

11

While You Wait...

While you wait, discover your God-given purpose, your true meaning for being here, for having been born, for being alive. The world needs what you have to offer! What are you good at? What do you love to do? I have heard it said, "If you can find a way to make a living doing what you love, you will never work a day in your life." Of course, nothing worth having ever comes easily. Actively getting involved and using your gifts and talents will open doors. Your gifts and talents will make room for you! In life, there are lots of waiting periods; waiting in traffic, waiting in lines, waiting for the doors of opportunity to open. Sometimes there are days that can drag on and on, some seemingly never ending, while other days can just fly by. Serving others will bring fulfillment and satisfaction when we are in those dreaded periods of waiting, when nothing seems to be happening or going right. We will be held accountable for our time here on earth. We need to use our time wisely. There is a honing that needs to be done—a refining of one's gifts, a working on and perfecting of the natural talents and abilities we were born with. When we actively get involved fulfilling our purpose in life, using our gifts and talents, we inevitably find our tribe—others who are also involved in their God-given purpose. This will breathe life into your dreams and bring energy to you. It will keep you on track, moving you in the direction of fulfilling your purpose.

There are lots of things in life that can sidetrack a person. Have you ever had a friend or significant other say something to you that made you feel less than great? Sometimes, the smallest thing can change the entire dynamic of a relationship. A guy and girl can be in a relationship, everything can be seemingly going fine, until one day the guy breaks up with the girl (or vice versa). Without warning, something can happen, causing one person or both people involved to not want to continue seeing the other. In such a lightly committed relationship that someone can get out of so easily by simply not returning a phone call, why would one want to give everything they have to offer to someone who could walk away from them at the drop of a hat? The only one that deserves your all, the emotional and physical part of you, everything you have to give, is the one that you're walking down the aisle toward on your wedding day. The one who is waiting there as you walk toward him is the one, and only one, that deserves all of you. At the altar is where he will begin to give his all to you, and you will begin to share your all with him. He is waiting down at the altar for his future bride, waiting to start building a life together.

That person is the only one that deserves a girl's all. Until that time, place your heart and future into God's hands. It is safe there. When you find you need a hug and no one is there, talk to God, sing, and cry out to Him. He sees you. He hears you. He knows you. He loves you. Hebrews 23:5c (KJB) states that God will never leave nor forsake you. He is always there. He's got you! Thank Him. In this life, when you find that you need a bit of refreshing, remember that being a blessing—sowing a seed of kindness toward another—will bring that blessing and refreshing right back to you!

About the Author

Bonnie Moubarak was born in Detroit, Michigan, where she attended parochial school.

Printed in the USA
CPSIA information can be obtained
at www.ICGtesting.com
LVHW080439040823
754031LV00016B/917

9 798887 385419